LONDON 2012 OLYMPIC VENUES
by James Nixon

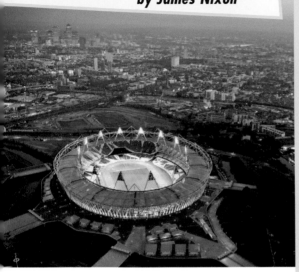

CONTENTS

Editor: Lynn Peppas
Proofreader: Crystal Sikkens
Editorial director:
   Kathy Middleton
**Print and production
   coordinator**: Katherine Berti
Cartoons by: John Alston
Photo research: James Nixon
Produced for Crabtree Publishing
Company by Discovery Books.

Picture Credits:
t=top, m = middle, b=bottom, l=left, r=right, OFC=outside front cover, OBC=outside back cover,
IFC=inside front cover; Getty Images: pp. 9 t, 26 t (Bryn Lennon); London 2012: OFC, pp. 2 b, 3 b, 4,
6, 8 b, 10 b, 16, 17 b, 20 b, 25, 27 m and b; Photoshot: pp. 12, 13 t (David Wimsett); Shutterstock: pp. 2
t (Antonio Abrignani), 3 t (Cosmin Manci), 3 b (AISPIX by Image Source), 5 t (dutourdumonde), 5 b
(mary416), 7 t (goldenangel), 9 b (Domenic Gareri), 10 b (EcoPrint), 14 t (Diego Barbieri), 15
(piotrwzk), 17 t (Nagy Melinda), 18 (yampi), 19 t (Laura Stone), 21 t (Oliver Sved), 24 t (Stephen
Mulcahey), 26 b (Jandrie Lombard), 27 t (Nick Hawkes); Wikimedia: 7 b (Andreas Levers), 8 t (Armin
Kuebelbeck), 11 t (J. Bar), 11 b (Fernando Pasculло), 13 b (Carlbob.com), 14 m (Stig Morten Skjaeran),
14 b (Senseiich), 19 b (David Hawgood), 20 t (Paddy Briggs), 21 b (Squeaky Knees), 22, 23 b
(Hawaiian Mama), 24 b (Doc Searls)

Library and Archives Canada Cataloguing in Publication

Nixon, James, 1982-
   London 2012 : Olympic venues / James Nixon.

(The Olympic sports)
Includes index.
Issued also in electronic formats.
ISBN 978-0-7787-4008-7 (bound).--ISBN 978-0-7787-4009-4 (pbk.)

   1. Olympic Games (30th : 2012 : London, England)--Juvenile
literature. 2. Paralympics (14th : 2012 : London, England)--
Juvenile literature. I. Title. II. Series: Olympic sports (St.
Catharines, Ont.)

GV722.2012N59 2012   j796.48   C2012-902463-5

Library of Congress Cataloging-in-Publication Data

Nixon, James, 1982-
London 2012 : Olympic venues / James Nixon.
p. cm. -- (The Olympic sports)
Includes index.
ISBN 978-0-7787-4008-7 (reinforced lib. bdg. : alk. paper) --
ISBN 978-0-7787-4009-4 (pbk. : alk. paper) -- ISBN 978-1-4271-7936-4
(electronic pdf) -- ISBN 978-1-4271-8051-3 (electronic html)
1. Olympic Games (30th : 2012 : London, England)--Juvenile literature.
2. Paralympics (30th : 2012 : London, England)--Juvenile literature.
I. Title.

GV7222012 .N59 2012
796.48--dc23

                                        2012015304

Crabtree Publishing Company
www.crabtreebooks.com   1-800-387-7650

Printed in Canada/052012/AV20120110

Published in Canada
Crabtree Publishing
616 Welland Ave.
St. Catharines, Ontario
L2M 5V6

Published in the United States
Crabtree Publishing
PMB 59051
350 Fifth Avenue, 59th Floor
New York, New York 10118

Published in the United Kingdom
Crabtree Publishing
Maritime House
Basin Road North, Hove
BN41 1WR

Published in Australia
Crabtree Publishing
3 Charles Street
Coburg North
VIC 3058

ALL EYES ON LONDON

In 2012, London will host the Summer Olympic Games for the third time in Olympic history. Will this Olympics prove to be as eventful as the previous two?

PREVIOUS OLYMPICS

In 1908, the Olympic Games were supposed to take place in Rome. The eruption of Mount Vesuvius in 1906, near Naples, required Italy's government to spend money on cleaning up the damage instead. London stepped in to host the Games.

After a twelve-year gap caused by World War II, London again hosted the Olympics in 1948. Due to the harsh post-war economy, no new venues could be built for these Games.

Vesuvius

A NEW IDEA

In 1948, a German doctor named Dr. Ludwig Guttmann created a separate competition for injured World War II soldiers at Stoke Mandeville Hospital, in England. Veterans from various sports clubs and hospitals competed with each other. The Stoke Mandeville Games held in Rome in 1960 were considered to be the first official **Paralympic Games**.

Olympic stadium in London

THE OLYMPIC PARK

During the 2012 Olympics, many events will be staged in a newly built Olympic Park in the east part of London. As well as containing sporting venues, it will house all the athletes. Some of the events will take place at other venues both inside and outside London.

DID YOU KNOW?

❦ The Olympic Village will contain 17,320 bedrooms. The dining hall will cater for 5,500 athletes at a time.

❦ After the Olympics, the Park will be known as Queen Elizabeth Olympic Park to celebrate the British Queen's 60th year on the throne.

SAVE THE NEWT

Ten thousand newts had to be relocated to a nature reserve from the area where the Olympic Park was built.

Swimming in Hyde Park

SEE THE SIGHTS

Long-distance races in the 2012 Olympics will pass some of London's most famous landmarks. Hampton Court Palace will be the site for the road cycling **time trial**. The grand palace is the former home of King Henry VIII. The marathon starts and finishes on the Mall, a road which runs between Buckingham Palace and Trafalgar Square. Hyde Park, London's biggest park, hosts the triathlon, where competitors will begin the race by swimming through the Serpentine Lake before they cycle and then run to the finish.

Hampton Court Palace

THE OLYMPIC STADIUM

The Olympic Stadium will be the centerpiece of the 2012 Games. The opening and closing ceremonies will be held there as well as the track and field events.

DURING THE GAMES

Spectators will have to cross pedestrian bridges to get into the stadium as it is on an island surrounded by waterways. Inside the stadium is a 262-foot (80 m) warm-up track and more than 700 rooms including changing rooms, medical suites, and prayer halls. A 66-foot (20 m) high, polythene wrap decorated with past sporting champions and countries' flags will encircle the stadium.

REDUCE AND RECYCLE

To avoid using up too many resources, the Olympic Stadium is the most **sustainable** ever built. It was constructed using much less steel and **carbon** than other stadiums. It features a low-carbon concrete recycled from industrial waste. The top ring of the stadium was built using spare gas pipes. Less steel was needed because the lower section of the stadium sits within a bowl in the ground.

DID YOU KNOW?

During the Olympics, the stadium will seat up to 80,000 people. The upper tier holding 55,000 seats is temporary and can be removed after the Games.

Olympic Stadium

PIGEONS KEEP OUT!

A hawk named Willow flies around the stadium to frighten off pigeons looking for nesting sites in the stadium.

London pigeon

Bird's Nest Stadium, Beijing

BEIJING 2008

The National Stadium in Beijing wowed spectators and viewers during the 2008 Olympics. Its complex arrangement of steel beams gives the stadium its nickname the "Bird's Nest." At one point 17,000 construction workers were building the stadium. Recently the stadium has been turned into a snow-theme park.

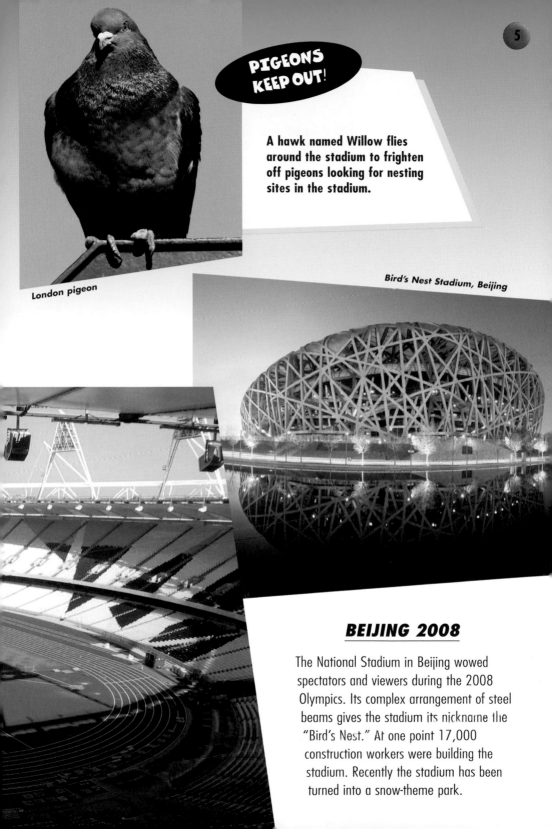

THE AQUATICS CENTRE

The first venue visitors will see as they enter the Olympic Park will be the stylish looking Aquatics Centre. Inside are two 164-foot (50 m) swimming pools and an 82-foot (25 m) diving pool.

DARING DESIGN

The Aquatics Centre's wave-like roof is 525 feet (160 m) long and up to 262 feet (80 m) wide, making it the same size as one and a half soccer fields. The design is unique. The 3,086-ton (2,800-metric ton) roof rests on just two concrete supports at each end. Inside, the roof is lined with 118,403 square feet (11,000 square meters) of recycled aluminum.

SAVING WATER

To reduce the amount of water used in the Aquatics Centre, old pool water will be reused to flush the venue's toilets.

Aquatics Centre

DID YOU KNOW?

*Hungary has won gold in the men's **water polo** at the last three Olympic Games and has won nine times in total.*

DURING THE GAMES

The Aquatics Centre will have a seating capacity of 17,500. The majority of spectators will be seated in two temporary wings that will be taken down after the Games. As well as swimming and diving, spectators can also watch the synchronized swimming, which is a cross between swimming, dance, and gymnastics. The water polo competition will be held in a temporary arena next door to the Aquatics Centre.

Berlin Outdoor Swimming Stadium

OUTDOOR SWIMMING

Before 1908, Olympic swimming events took place in a river or lake. Indoor swimming was not seen until the London Olympics in 1948. Berlin's outdoor swimming stadium used in the 1936 Olympics is still in use today. The changing rooms are located under the stands.

HAND ALL AND BASKET ALL

Basketball and handball are two team sports that will be held in the Olympic Park. The Basketball Arena is a temporary structure. Handball will be held in a venue called the Copper Box.

THE COPPER BOX

The Copper Box was finished in May 2011. It is coated with 32,292 square feet (3,000 square meters) of recycled copper. As the copper ages it will develop a rich, natural color. At ground level the building has glass walls, and visitors to the Olympic Park will be able to watch the handball taking place inside. The venue has a vibrant and colorful interior that will be illuminated at night through the glazed walls.

Handball

Vibrant Copper Box interior

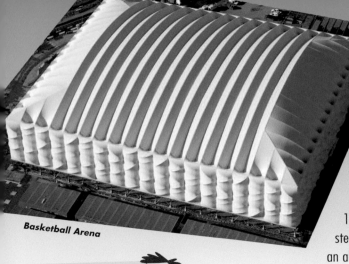

Basketball Arena

THE BASKETBALL ARENA

The Basketball Arena is the largest temporary venue ever built for an Olympic Games. It took 15 months to erect the 1,102-ton (1000-metric ton), steel-framed building. The doors are an above average 8 feet (2.4 m) high, to accommodate the extra-tall basketball players. It is hoped that the venue will be reassembled somewhere else in the UK when the Games have finished.

DID YOU KNOW?

The average height for an NBA basketball player is over 6 feet 6 inches (2 m) tall!

DURING THE GAMES

The Copper Box will host handball up until the quarter-final stage. The semifinals and final will be held in the larger Basketball Arena. There will be just 22 hours to turn the basketball field into a handball field with goals at each end instead of basketball hoops. During the Paralympics, the Basketball Arena will be used for wheelchair rugby and basketball. There will be just 12 hours to get the rugby field ready after the wheelchair basketball finishes.

SAVING LIGHT

The Copper Box has 88 light pipes installed in the ceiling that draw sunlight into the venue. This will reduce the amount of light energy needed by 40 percent.

Basketball

THE RIVERBANK ARENA

The temporary Riverbank Arena inside the Olympic Park has two separate fields. It is here that the Olympic field hockey and Paralympic 5-a-side soccer competitions will be played.

DURING THE GAMES

The Riverbank Arena is expected to host over 780,000 spectators during the 2012 Games. To reflect the color scheme of London 2012 the playing field area is blue and the surrounding parts are pink. The balls will be colored yellow as this color contrasts well with the blue and can easily be seen by the spectators.

DID YOU KNOW?

It will be the first time that Olympic field hockey and Paralympic soccer will be played on a different colored surface from the traditional green.

Field hockey at the Riverbank Arena

Greyhound racing

GOING TO THE DOGS

The Riverbank Arena's fields are built on the site of a former greyhound racing stadium.

Sydney Hockey Centre

HOCKEY HISTORY

In 1976, field hockey became the first sport to be played on artificial turf in the Olympics. The matches were played at the Molson Stadium in Montreal, a ground normally used in the Canadian Football League. For the Sydney 2000 Olympics, a new and permanent hockey center was built (above). The stadium's roof resembles a soaring glider. It is held up by one mast, removing any need for columns that would block the spectators' view of the field.

VOLLEYBALL

It was originally planned that the Olympic Park would also contain a new volleyball arena. However, the volleyball tournament will now be held in Earls Court Exhibition Centre. The center holds hundreds of events each year from conferences to live music. Athletes will have to travel 11 miles (18 kilometers) across London from the Olympic Village to reach Earls Court.

Earls Court

THE VELOPARK

The Velopark is at the northern end of the Olympic Park. It contains the Velodrome for track cycling and a BMX track that will be used during and after the Games.

THE VELODROME

The design of the Velodrome reflects the shape and curves of the racetrack inside. It has been nicknamed "The Pringle" by some because of its similarity to the potato chip. The foundations for the stadium had to be driven up to 85 feet (26 m) into the ground to provide stability because the venue is built on top of a 100-year-old landfill site.

FAST TRACK

The track in the Velodrome has been designed with the aim of making it the fastest in the world. It is made from 35 miles (56 km) of Siberian pine wood fixed into place with more than 350,000 nails!

ECODROME

The Velodrome is the most sustainable in the Olympic Park. The wood has been sourced from sustainable forests. Skylights reduce the need for electric lighting. The ventilation system is also completely natural, removing the need for air conditioning. The cable net roof structure is more than twice as light as the Beijing Velodrome's.

DID YOU KNOW?

British cyclist Sir Chris Hoy won two golds on the cycling track in Beijing in 2008. He was involved in the design process for London's Velodrome and will be competing again in 2012.

Velodrome exterior

Velodrome interior

BMX TRACK

The BMX track will seat 6,000 people during the Games. The track is 1,542 feet (470 m) long for men and 1,411 feet (430 m) for women. The series of ramps, bends, and jumps on the course have made it one of the most challenging BMX tracks ever.

BMX track

THE EXCEL LONDON

Outside of the Olympic Park, events will be staged at existing venues. The ExCeL center in London's Docklands is staging more Olympic and Paralympic sports than any other venue.

DURING THE GAMES

The ExCeL building will be divided into five sporting arenas for the Games, each holding over 5,000 spectators. In the Olympics it will be used for boxing, **fencing**, judo, **tae kwon do**, table tennis, weightlifting, and wrestling. During the Paralympics it will stage table tennis, **boccia**, judo, power lifting, wheelchair fencing, and sitting volleyball. In total, 154 gold medals will be won at this venue.

Boccia

TOUCHÉ

Fencing is one of four sports that has featured at every modern Olympic Games. Competitors in fencing traditionally shout touché (French for "touched") when they are hit by their opponent.

ExCeL London

ABOUT EXCEL

The ExCeL opened in 2000. It is one of Europe's largest exhibition spaces and is extremely versatile. The venue has been used for fashion and motor shows, concerts, political **summits**, award ceremonies, and auditions for the TV shows *X Factor* and *Britain's Got Talent*. High profile boxing and wrestling matches have been held here previously, too.

1960 ROME OLYMPICS

In 1960, the wrestling events were held at the Basilica of Maxentius, the largest building in the ruins of the ancient Roman Forum. Wrestlers from Turkey did very well, winning seven of the 16 gold medals on offer. The Forum was the center of public life in ancient Rome, and staged public speeches, criminal trials, and fights between gladiators. The south and central sections of the Basilica were probably destroyed by an earthquake in 847 CE.

Roman Forum with the arches of the Basilica of Maxentius (top left)

DID YOU KNOW?

The ExCeL covers 699, 654 square feet (65,000 square meters) and is the largest hall without columns in Europe.

GREENWICH PARK

The equestrian events in 2012 will be held in Greenwich Park, London's oldest Royal Park. The park, which has views over the River Thames and central London, dates back to 1433. It is now a World Heritage Site.

DURING THE GAMES

Greenwich Park was chosen because of its closeness to the Olympic Village. Competitors will feel they are at the heart of the Olympic action. The main arena is a temporary structure that seats 23,000 people. It will host **dressage** and show jumping. In the cross-country event, spectators will be able to walk around the park, stopping to watch horses pass over particular jumps. All structures will be taken down after the Games.

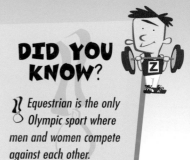

DID YOU KNOW?

Equestrian is the only Olympic sport where men and women compete against each other.

Cross-country in Greenwich Park

LONG DISTANCE GAMES

In 1956, the equestrian events were held in Stockholm, Sweden. This is despite the Olympics taking place on the other side of the world in Melbourne, Australia! Australia had quarantine rules at the time, which meant that horses were not allowed into the country.

HORSE GUARDS PARADE

The beach volleyball competition will take place near the British Prime Minister's doorstep at Horse Guards Parade. Soldiers at Horse Guards Parade provide protection for the queen. The parade ground is famous for the Trooping of the Color ceremony on the Queen's official birthday in June. When the Olympics are over, the guards will move back into place.

ON THE BEACH

To make a beach volleyball competition possible, 120 truckloads of sand had to be imported to Horse Guards Parade. There is enough sand for one competition court, two warm-up courts, and two training courts. After the event, the sand will be donated to sports centers across London so that they can set up their own beach volleyball courts and encourage young people to take up the sport.

Beach volleyball at Horse Guards Parade

...IG STADIUMS

The North Greenwich Arena is the largest indoor arena in London and is set to host gymnastics in 2012. Soccer games will be played at Wembley Stadium, the largest sporting venue of any kind in the UK.

North Greenwich Arena

DID YOU KNOW?

♫ After the millennium celebrations passed, the British government faced an embarrassing situation. The Millennium Dome was costing them over 1,500,000 US dollars (1,000,000 UK pounds) per month to maintain and they did not know what to do with it.

THE NORTH GREENWICH ARENA

Originally built to celebrate the millennium in 2000, North Greenwich Arena has been transformed into a sports and entertainment arena. In 2008, the dome became the world's busiest music venue. Bon Jovi were the first act to ever play at the arena in 2007. In 2011, Rihanna performed 11 nights there, a record for a female solo artist. During the Games the venue will host the artistic and trampoline gymnastics, and the basketball finals, where the seating capacity will be 20,000.

Gymnast on pommel horse

ARTISTIC GYMNASTICS

The artistic gymnastics will draw large crowds to the North Greenwich Arena. It is always one of the most popular events at the Olympics. The grace, strength, and skill of the athletes is breathtaking to watch. The men battle for gold on the **pommel horse**, rings, floor, parallel bars, **vault**, and high bar. The women compete on the vault, uneven bars, floor, and balance beam.

WEMBLEY STADIUM

The soccer competition will be staged at six grounds across the UK. The finals will be played at the magnificent Wembley Stadium, which has a capacity of 90,000. The stadium's arch soars over 427 feet (130 m) into the sky and it comes complete with a sliding roof if the weather turns bad.

PERFECT 10

In the 1976 Montreal Olympics, 14-year-old Romanian Nadia Comaneci was scored ten out of ten by the judges for her performance on the uneven bars. It was the first time a perfect ten had been awarded in Olympic Games history.

Wembley Stadium

FAMOUS OLD VENUES

Two of the most historic and famous sporting venues in the world will be used in London 2012. Lord's Cricket Ground and the Wimbledon tennis courts will be part of the action.

Lord's Cricket Ground

Archery

LORD'S

Lord's has been a venue for international cricket since the late 1800s. Cricket has not been in the Olympics since 1904 so it will be the setting for the archery competitions instead. The archery range will be created on the outfield of the main ground. After the Games the archery equipment will be handed out to schools and clubs across the country.

ATHENS OLYMPICS

The Panathinaiko Stadium in Athens hosted the first modern Olympic Games in 1896. It is the only major stadium in the world built entirely of white marble. The running track follows the ancient model with hairpin bends at each end. In the 2004 Olympics in Athens, the old stadium was used again, this time for the archery events.

SHARP SHOOTERS

Archers aim to hit a gold bullseye measuring just 4.8 inches (12.2 cm) in diameter from a distance of 230 feet (70m)!

Wimbledon Centre Court

WIMBLEDON

Wimbledon has been the setting for the famous Wimbledon tennis tournament since 1877. Naturally it will be holding the Olympic tennis competitions in 2012. It is the only remaining major grass-court tennis venue in the world. It has, however, been modernized many times in its history. In 2009, Centre Court was given a sliding roof, so matches can continue even in wet weather.

DID YOU KNOW?

Wimbledon hosted Olympic tennis in 1908. The 2012 Olympics will be the first time Olympic tennis has been played on grass for 104 years.

OUTSIDE LONDON

The majority of the Olympics will take place in a small area in east London. Some events will be based outside London because they require special facilities or terrain.

SAILING

Weymouth Bay and Portland Harbour on the south coast of England will host the Olympic and Paralympic sailing competitions. The venue is 120 miles (193 km) from London, but provides one of the best natural sailing waters in the world. The harbor is exposed to reliable winds, but is sheltered from large waves by a strip of land called Chesil Beach. The site has held international sailing events before, and boasts world-class facilities.

DURING AND AFTER THE GAMES

The facilities at Weymouth and Portland have been enhanced for the Olympics. A permanent 820-foot (250 m) slipway and new mooring areas have been built. The state-of-the-art venue will be left behind for the local community after the Games. The sailing bay is a natural **amphitheater** and there are several viewing points for spectators to watch from, even if they do not have tickets. Or they can watch the action on a big screen on Weymouth Beach.

DID YOU KNOW?

A cruise liner docked at Portland Port will be used as accommodation for the sailing competitors.

Portland Harbour

2012 VENUES

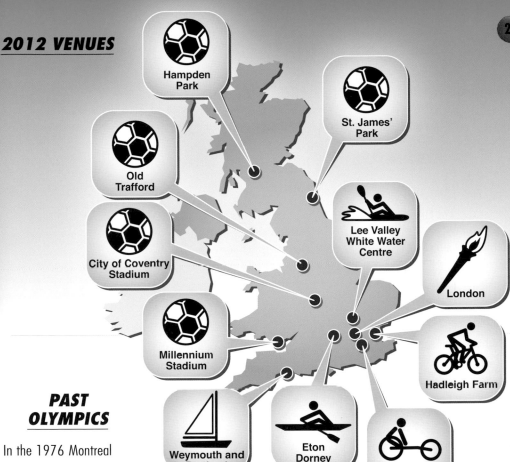

Hampden Park

St. James' Park

Old Trafford

City of Coventry Stadium

Lee Valley White Water Centre

London

Millennium Stadium

Hadleigh Farm

Weymouth and Portland

Eton Dorney

Brands Hatch

PAST OLYMPICS

In the 1976 Montreal Games, the sailing events took place on the Great Lakes in Kingston, Ontario. It was the first and only time that competitors sailed on freshwater. The 1992 Olympic sailing venue in Barcelona was probably the worst in history. The competitors complained of debris in the water including plastic bags, dead rats, and floating refrigerators! The port authorities had to send out four garbage vessels daily to collect the debris.

SAILING HERO

In 1988, Canadian sailor Lawrence Lemieux was in second place when he noticed Joseph Chan from Singapore in the water far from his boat, which had capsized. Lemieux abandoned his position to rescue his rival and ended up finishing the race last.

Sailing

ROWING AND CANOEING

Olympic champions will be crowned on the still-water lake at Eton Dorney and the white-water slalom course at Lee Valley. These venues for rowing and canoeing are just outside London.

ETON DORNEY

The lake at Eton Dorney near Windsor Castle was built for rowing and flat-water canoeing. The course is 7,218 feet (2,200 m) long and completely straight. It is split into eight lanes measuring 44.3 feet (13.5 m) wide, with a separate return lane added to the side. The existing facility will be upgraded to include 20,000 seats for Olympic spectators.

DID YOU KNOW?

The lake at Eton Dorney is owned by Eton College, a public school for boys founded by King Henry VI in 1440.

Eton College

Aerial shot of Eton Dorney

Canoe slalom at Lee Valley

SUPER STATS

The 984-foot (300 m) competition course at Lee Valley drops 16 feet (5 m) in height from start to finish. The pumps on the course create enough water to fill a 164-foot (50 m) swimming pool every minute!

LEE VALLEY

The canoe slalom competition will be held at the Lee Valley White Water Centre. It was officially opened in 2010 and became the first newly constructed venue to be completed. The rushing water on the 984-foot (300 m) course is created by a system of pumps which lift 3,434 gallons (13,000 liters) of water down the course every second! The white water is created by these pumps and obstacles placed on the course.

AFTER THE GAMES

The spectator seating at Lee Valley is only temporary, but the facilities will remain in place after the Olympics. The local community and visitors will be able to use the venue for canoeing and **kayaking**, whether they are beginners or elite-level athletes. The center will also become a major leisure attraction for those wanting to try white-water rafting.

CHANGING PLANS

The organizers of London 2012 had to make some changes to their original plans. The mountain bike course and the road cycling route both had to be moved because organizers were told the courses were not difficult enough.

MOUNTAIN BIKING

Mountain bike races are held on rough terrain and include rocky paths, tricky climbs, and difficult downhill sections. London 2012 originally planned to hold the event south of London in the Weald Country Park but it was not challenging enough for elite competitors. Now, Hadleigh Farm, east of London, will host the event. The 550-acre (223-hectare) course is specially built with extremely difficult features such as rock formations, zig-zag climbs, and steep drops.

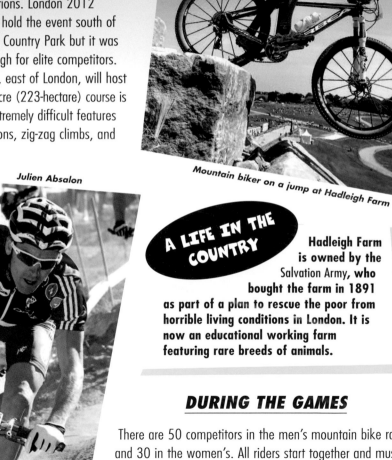

Mountain biker on a jump at Hadleigh Farm

Julien Absalon

A LIFE IN THE COUNTRY

Hadleigh Farm is owned by the Salvation Army, **who bought the farm in 1891** as part of a plan to rescue the poor from horrible living conditions in London. It is now an educational working farm featuring rare breeds of animals.

DURING THE GAMES

There are 50 competitors in the men's mountain bike race and 30 in the women's. All riders start together and must complete a set number of laps of the course. There are fabulous viewing points for spectators along the course as it winds its way through woods and parkland. The man to beat in the men's event is Frenchman Julien Absalon who won gold in 2004 and 2008 and is aiming for a **hat trick**.

Box Hill

THE OLYMPIC ROAD RACE

The cycling road-race route was also changed to make it tougher. Both the men and women will now head southwest out of London into the Surrey countryside. The men have to climb the punishing Box Hill nine times before they head back to London for the finish. Riders who want to win gold will have to beat Britain's Mark Cavendish, who is known as the "fastest man on two wheels."

Cavendish winning a 2012 road-race test event

Paralympian at Brands Hatch

DID YOU KNOW?

The Paralympic cycling road race is set to take place on the Brands Hatch motor racing circuit.

2012 OLYMPIC SCHEDULE

July/August	Wed 25	Thu 26	Fri 27	Sat 28	Sun 29	Mon 30	Tue 31	Wed 1	Thu 2
CEREMONIES			OC						
Archery			•	1	1	•	•	•	1
Athletics									
Badminton				•	•	•	•	•	•
Basketball				•	•	•	•	•	•
Boxing				•	•	•	•	•	•
Canoeing					•	•	1	1	2
Cycling				1	1			2	2
Diving					1	1	1	1	
Equestrian				•	•	•	2		•
Fencing				1	1	1	1	2	1
Field hockey					•	•	•	•	•
Gymnastics				•	•	1	1	1	1
Handball				•	•	•	•	•	•
Judo				2	2	2	2	2	2
Modern pentathlon									
Rowing				•	•	•	•	3	3
Sailing					•	•	•	•	•
Shooting				2	2	1	1	1	1
Soccer	•	•		•	•		•	•	
Swimming				4	4	4	4	4	4
Synchronized swimming									
Table tennis				•	•	•	•	1	1
Tae kwon do									
Tennis				•	•	•	•	•	•
Triathlon									
Volleyball				•	•	•	•	•	•
Water polo					•	•	•	•	•
Weightlifting				1	2	2	2	2	
Wrestling									
TOTAL GOLD MEDALS				12	14	12	15	20	18

Legend:

- **OC** Opening ceremony
- **•** Event competitions
- **1** Number of gold medals awarded
- **CC** Closing ceremony

	Fri 3	Sat 4	Sun 5	Mon 6	Tue 7	Wed 8	Thurs 9	Fri 10	Sat 11	Sun 12	Gold Medals
										CC	
	1										4
	2	5	7	5	4	4	5	6	8	1	47
	1	2	2								5
	•	•	•	•	•	•	•	•	1	1	2
	•	•	•	•	•	•	3	•	5	5	13
				•	•	4	4	•	4		16
	2	1	1	1	3	•	•	2	1	1	18
	•	•	1	•	1	•	1	•	1		8
	•	•	•	1	1	2					6
	1	1	1								10
	•	•	•	•	•	•	•	1	1		2
	1	1	3	3	4		•	•	1	1	18
	•	•	•	•	•	•	•	•	1	1	2
	2										14
									1	1	2
	4	4									14
	•	•	2	2	2	1	1	1	1		10
	2	2	1	2							15
	•	•		•	•		1	•	1		2
	4	4						1	1		34
			•	•	1		•	1			2
	•	•	•	•	1	1					4
						2	2	2	2		8
	•	2	3								5
		1			1						2
	•	•	•	•	•	1	1	•	1	1	4
	•	•	•	•	•	•	1	•		1	2
	2	1	1	1	1						15
			2	3	2	2	2	2	3	2	18
	22	**24**	**24**	**18**	**21**	**17**	**22**	**16**	**32**	**15**	**302**

2012 PARALYMPIC SCHEDULE

OC	Opening ceremony
•	Event competitions
1	Number of gold medals awarded
CC	Closing ceremony

August/September	Wed 29	Thu 30	Fri 31	Sat 1	Sun 2	Mon 3	Tue 4	Wed 5	Thu 6	Fri 7	Sat 8	Sun 9	Gold Medals
CEREMONIES	OC											CC	
Archery		•	•	•	•	4	3	2					9
Athletics			11	17	20	17	21	20	21	16	23	4	170
Boccia					•	•	3	•	•	•	4		7
Cycling	5	5	5	3				18	4	6	4		50
Equestrian		•	•	2	3	2	4						11
Goalball		•	•	•	•	•	•	•	•	2			2
Judo		4	4	5									13
Powerlifting	2	3	3	3	3	3	3						20
Rowing			•	•	4								4
Sailing				•	•	•	•	•	3				3
Shooting	2	2	2	1	1	1	1	2					12
Soccer 5-a-side			•	•	•	•	•	•	•	•	1		1
Soccer 7-a-side			•	•	•	•	•	•	•	•		1	1
Swimming	15	15	15	14	14	15	15	15	15	15			148
Table tennis		•	•	•	11	10	•	•	•	4	4		29
Volleyball		•	•	•	•	•	•	•	•	1	1		2
Wheelchair basketball		•	•	•	•	•	•	•	•	1	1		2
Wheelchair fencing							4	4	2	1	1		12
Wheelchair rugby								•	•	•	•	1	1
Wheelchair tennis				•	•	•	•	1	•	2	3		6
TOTAL GOLD MEDALS	28	40	49	59	51	54	64	47	48	57	6		503

GLOSSARY

amphitheater A round arena where sporting events take place in a central space surrounded by spectators

boccia A game where competitors throw leather balls as close as they can to a white target ball

capsize Overturn a boat in the water

carbon A chemical element which in its pure form is found in diamonds

dressage A horse riding event where competitors have to demonstrate smooth movements and horse obedience

equestrian Horse riding

fencing The sport of fighting with swords according to a set of rules

handball A team game similar to soccer but in which the ball is thrown or hit with the hands rather than kicked

hat trick Achieving the same thing three times in a row

kayak A type of light canoe with a small opening in the top to sit in

Paralympic Games An international athletics competition for athletes with disabilities, which takes place after the Olympic Games every four years

pommel horse An apparatus with plastic handles that gymnasts use to do swings of the legs and body

quarantine The isolation of certain animals or people to prevent the spread of something, such as a disease

Salvation Army A Christian organization noted for its work helping the poor

slalom A sporting event with a winding course marked out by obstacles

summit A meeting between heads of government

sustainable If you do something in a sustainable way you are conserving the environment and not using up natural resources

tae kwon do A martial art similar to karate

time trial A test of a competitor's speed against the clock over a set distance

vault A gymnastic apparatus where contestants use a springboard and a table to perform a somersault

water polo A seven-a-side game in which swimmers try to throw a ball into the opponent's net

World Heritage Site A place that is listed as a site of special cultural or physical significance

FIND OUT MORE

www.london2012.com
The official website of the 2012 Olympic and Paralympic Games.

www.olympic.org
This website of the International Olympic Committee lets you relive past Olympic Games as well as giving you the latest news.

www.guardian.co.uk/sport/series/london-2012-60-second-expert-guides-to-olympic-events
A quick guide showing you the rules and tactics in Olympic sports.

www.visitlondon.com/london2012/venues
Information, images, and maps on the 2012 Olympic venues.

INDEX